Jargon 50

The Appalachian Photographs of Doris Ulmann

Remembrance by *John Jacob Niles*

Preface by *Jonathan Williams*

THE JARGON SOCIETY, *Penland, North Carolina* 1971

This project is supported by a grant from the *National Endowment for the Arts* in Washington, D.C., a Federal agency created by Act of Congress in 1965.

Further assistance from the *Mary Duke Biddle Foundation* (New York City) and the *John Wesley and Anna Hodgin Hanes Foundation* (Winston-Salem) has been crucial.

The generous co-operation of *Berea College*, the *Doris Ulmann Foundation*, and Mr. John Jacob Niles is here gratefully acknowledged.

The frontispiece is a photograph of Doris Ulmann by John Jacob Niles.

The end-papers, from an Appalachian coverlet, are courtesy of the *Smithsonian Institution's* photographic service and Mr. Anthony Landreau of the *Textile Museum.*

"They All Want To Go
And Dress Up"

Hamlin Garland once quoted Doris Ulmann's remark (above) and went on to say: "It is not an easy task to induce a farmer's wife to have her picture taken in her kitchen gown peeling potatoes." It is precisely this ability to capture the old farmland-potato style—earthy, yet savory—that distinguishes the Ulmann photographs and puts them in a great realist tradition. A tradition, apparently, known to almost no photographer of the present, let it be said. Ever since *Mnemosyne and the Muses* became a rock-group franchise and moved into a commune near Tabula Rasa, Arkansas, the profession includes multitudes with foreheads villainously low. However, we will surely learn to go to Doris Ulmann's hundreds of prints of the Southern Appalachians at their date in history (the late 1920's and early 1930's) as we have learned to go to John Jacob Niles for his discoveries of mountain folk-ballad. It is an apt thing, that they were traveling companions. Miss Ulmann gives us a dated record of a particular home-place; she does so with sufficient art that Julia Cameron, Alvin Langdon Coburn, Atget, and Lartigue are some of the names with whom I would like to link her. I'd like to be at dinner with all of them one evening in Viper, Kentucky—with plenty of applejack, plenty of Maker's Mark, plenty of Johnny Niles' home-cured ham, plenty of beaten biscuits. I doubt that the talk would get very loud. Nobody but me would bring up topics from the dark side of rustication, like Marx's notion of the idiocy of rural life; or, that chilling sentence from James Dickey's novel, *Deliverance:* "There is always something wrong with people in the country."

Doris Ulmann said: "...I have been more deeply moved by some of my mountaineers than by any literary person. A face that has the marks of having lived intensely, that expresses some phase of life, some dominant quality or intellectual power, constitutes for me an interesting face. For this reason the face of an older person, perhaps not beautiful in the strictest sense, is usually more appealing than the face of a younger person who has scarcely been touched by life."

It is useful to compare Miss Ulmann's straightforward portraiture and its somewhat wistful tone of reverie with what came immediately after her—the *Farm Security Administration*, Roy Stryker, Walker Evans, et al. She is not about to give us "the dream in the peasant's bent shoulders." A person of her alien refinement, photographing proud country people, would have considered that an invasion of privacy. One kind of vision should not obliterate another. Meaning: the art of the quiet is no less than public yelling and propaganda. Most of the persons in the Ulmann photographs—for all their character and handicraft—are 'sociologically redundant,' but that is hardly the point. Ah, what to do with 'modesty' persons? As Molly Kirkbride, a famous non-electronic knitter of Wensleydale, Yorkshire, once said: "Remember, we were nobbut browt up like bullocks." The faces in this book are far from bestial, for all of that. It is sad to think of them as statistics in some icy governmental report on Poverty Pockets. Doris Ulmann wanted the photographs to show the existence of a rural handicraft movement and to suggest that a number of mountain men and women could get by on their own with a market for their goods. She said to John Jacob Niles: "Johnny, you're a poet, you don't need much. Poets don't need much. If you overpay them they stop being poets." Underpay a craftsman and a poet, the result is the same: a vestigial occupation, a disappearing people, scorned by the Middle-Class as hillbillies and as freaks.

John Jacob Niles has written in the warm, rambling reminiscence that follows a unique account of his companionship with Doris Ulmann. It must have been a tiresome, and heart-breaking, task, and he confided: "You young men who enjoy the health of youth cannot imagine what this has done to me." Still, it was his story to tell, even after forty years. It is too important to be lost under the latest onslaught of groovy kidstuff. I hear Ringo's just bought himself some Levis and a corncob pipe full of dope and gone to Nashville to cut some country-soul. How was it *Time* defined a folksinger? Anyone who makes more than $15,000 a year singing through his nose.

The Doris Ulmann biography is a brief one. She was born in New York City in 1884. She was educated in public school; later at the School of Ethical Culture and Columbia University. She studied photography with Clarence H. White.

Johns Hopkins University published her book of *Portraits of the Medical Faculty of the Johns Hopkins University* in 1922; in 1925 Rudge issued *A Portrait Gallery of American Editors*. But, her major published works are the following: *Roll, Jordan, Roll*, seventy portraits of the Negro in South Carolina, with a text by Julia Peterkin (Ballou, 1933); and *Handicrafts of the Southern Highlands*, fifty-eight illustrations taken especially for a text by the late Allen H. Eaton (Russell Sage Foundation, New York, 1937). The latter is a particularly important book and it is hoped that rumors of a reprint by Dover Books are soon realized. Allen Eaton, like Horace Kephart, did marvelous work in behalf of the southern mountains and their people. His support of Doris Ulmann's endeavor is second only to J. J. Niles'.

When Doris Ulmann died at the age of 50 in New York City on August 28, 1934, there was a modest obituary in the *Times*. Little had been written about her or her photographs. In the *Bookman* (#72) she was interviewed by Dale Warren. Hamlin Garland wrote a piece in the July 1927 issue of *The Mentor*. In *Theatre Arts Monthly* (February 1930), there was an article: "The Stuff of American Drama in Photographs by Doris Ulmann." I have been unable to locate anything else until an issue of *The Call Number* (Spring 1958), published by the Library of the University of Oregon at Eugene. Here we have a transcription from a tape-recording by John Jacob Niles called "Doris Ulmann: Preface and Recollections;" a note on the photographic collection of her prints and glass negatives in the Library by Allen Eaton (an alumnus); and a vita by Alfred Heilpern.

Now is the time to explain how the selection of photographs was made and to thank the many people who have been of great help along the way. First, it was an assignment from Rose Slivka, Editor of *Craft Horizons*, that led me to Berea, Kentucky in the spring of 1965 to begin research on a long article on the Southern Appalachians. While attending a conference of the *Southern Highland Handicraft Guild*, someone in the Art Department of Berea College (Jim . . . . — such are the power of memory and gratitude) asked me if I'd like to see a bunch of old photographs of mountain people kept in the basement. That was the first quick glimpse of the Ulmann Archive, enough to fix it in my mind. The next development was in Lexington, Kentucky, spring

1967 (after a long sojourn in Great Britain). I was the guest of Rena and John Jacob Niles for a fine Sunday brunch out at Boot Hill Farm. JJN got to talking about the Ulmann photographs and the idea of a book made itself very clear and insistent. He's an infectious character, full of that countrified arrogance I carry around myself in ample measure. I was all for a book too, right then. All we needed was a *lot* of money. Since you are holding this volume in your hands, that means that after three drab years, we finally got it—from the two sources identified a few pages back.

But, to go back: on one of my poetry-reading, snake-oil-dispensing sessions at Berea College in late 1967, I took off a day to go through thousands of Doris Ulmann prints in the vaults. I picked 81. Then I asked Ralph Eugene Meatyard to drive down from Lexington and have an independent run-through. He chose 251, some of which duplicated my own. The total 300 then went to New York City, where they were scrutinized by non-blue-grass-eyes at the offices of *Aperture*—eyes belonging to Minor White, Lyle Bongé, Michael Hoffman, and Emanuel Navaretta. The final 63 plates are our collective responsibility. I am amused that Gene Meatyard and I, used to mountain folk all our lives, let one bunch of outlanders in: plate 33, who turn out to be three shrimp fishermen from around Mobile, Alabama, according to Johnny Niles. Let them stand for the Great American Gumbo, making the eyes water and the mind multiple…One other peculiarity: we unknowingly selected a number of persons from the Brasstown Community of North Carolina. It was surely a distinguished place. And it wasn't many miles away that Niles wrote that superb song, "I Wonder As I Wander."

Berea College could not have been more cooperative about our use of its Ulmann print legacy. Our thanks to President Willis Weatherford and, in particular, to Lester F. Pross, Dorothy Tredennick and Harry Segedy of the Art Department. They have been most indulgent over the delays and miseries of book production…Bill Schafer, in the English Department, is another friend who has been of constant use and enthusiasm in this project.

Besides Johnny and Rena Niles, who have been closest to Doris Ulmann and this publication, Kentucky has produced other advocates: the late Tom Merton; Gene Meatyard, Guy Davenport, Wendell Berry, Mrs. Victor Hammer, and Jonathan Greene.

In the Special Collections Department of the University of Oregon Library (which houses the other major Ulmann collection besides Berea), Martin Schmitt has been especially cordial both in correspondence and when I visited Eugene to see the glass negatives.

In North Carolina I do not forget the abiding help of the following: Philip and Joan Hanes, Douglas and Emily Lewis, John Ehle, Bill Brown of Penland School, Bill Baskin, Sue Moore, and Mrs. James H. Semans.

Michael Hoffman, of *Aperture*, deserves advance asphodels for much valuable work on production and for securing the design services of Sam Maitin.

The last thing to say is that all of us hope this book will do justice to a remarkable woman's remarkable work. She has had to wait too long.

Jonathan Williams
Corn Close, Dentdale, Yorkshire

Doris Ulmann: As I Remember Her

Doris Ulmann loved people, particularly when they were engaged in some form of productive labor—fruit-peddlers in Bleecker Street, New York City, men curing hides in North Carolina, brick-layers, nurses with prams, symphony-orchestra players, weavers and spinners, grand-opera singers, play-actors of all colors and ages, cotton-pickers in the Deep South, doctors and lawyers everywhere....Doris loved people, particularly when they were at work.

It was through her interest in the theatre that I met her. She had stayed away from the Broadway playhouses and come all the way down to the Grand Street Theatre to see a performance of "The Dybbuk." But "The Dybbuk" was still in rehearsal, so she and her party settled for the Grand Street Follies.

I was playing three parts in the Follies that year—Abie in a burlesque version of "Abie's Irish Rose," a Spanish card-player in a short number, the title which escapes me, and Woodrow Wilson in a skit about him. Somehow through the make-up, the lights and the scenery, Doris Ulmann saw exactly what she had been wanting for a long while—an active, youngish man with a strong back and what she hoped were strong arms, a man with an accent that sounded faintly like the southern mountaineers she had met, but best of all, a vagabond type who was ready and willing for any kind of novel experience, and a ballad-singer, to boot. (One should remember that folk-ballad singers, in those long-ago days, were not found hiding under every mulberry bush—I am talking now about the late 1920's.)

I cannot remember whether I gave up the Follies or whether the Follies gave me up, but I do know that a short while later, I was sitting up until the small hours of those hot New York City summer nights, reading to Doris or listening to her read the German classics (which she did quite wonderfully). Of course, I ran endless errands for her and cooked up innumerable pots of coffee, and meanwhile I was watching and studying the fascinating process of photography.

My ex-aviator friends (I had flown in World War I) said: "Hunky, why don't you give up this night-time photography business, come out with us and live some life?" That was over 40 years ago, and now most of them have disappeared, and I am still living some life and having my own kind of fun.

As a very young girl, Doris Ulmann developed a stomach-ulcer, and although she went through several sieges of corrective surgery, she never completely recovered. Why her doctors permitted her to drink such quantities of very strong black coffee is something I never discovered. But coffee and soup were the things she took most willingly, meanwhile smoking in the best chain-smoker manner.

She stood $5'4\frac{1}{2}''$ tall and never weighed over 105 pounds. She moved with a quiet kind of grace and always wore the loveliest clothes, even when we were in the backwoods of Eastern Kentucky.

At home, at 1000 Park Avenue in New York City, she was able to get a proper diet, but away from home, during the six to eight months she spent each year in the Southern Appalachians, it was impossible to feed her adequately. The food procurable there, in the late 1920's and early 1930's, was the world's worst—and most of it was fried. To counteract this situation, I carried a provision-box, and with the help of kindly hotel cooks, we managed somehow. Of course, the colleges and schools with whom we worked were most cooperative. But I used to look at Doris and wonder how much longer she could hold out against her physical problems.

Black-bean soup pleased her greatly, and it fell to me to visit a little delicatessen in the 80's not far from Second Avenue to purchase the black beans. Then I had to teach her personal cooks how to cook them and how to serve the soup with a slice of lemon, a slice of hard-boiled egg and a generous dollop of sherry. Doris loved it and would have it over and over again, if only the black beans could be found. Then Macy's put in a supply, and that made matters simpler.

Doris loved stewed fruit, and, as a matter of record, I think I can say she never ate any raw fruit except avocado pears. She seldom ate coarse bread (again, her ulcer), but I believe I might have gotten her in the habit of cooked cereal, some cracked wheat and steel-cut oats if I had had time. I did finally find a kind of re-ground whole wheat, which was made into bread in her own kitchen. She affectionately named it "Johnnie's bread."

Whenever I was in her home at breakfast-time, we ate at a very small table, so small that she could reach over and pat me lightly on the face when I sliced her a piece of this wonderful bread, which was made with some sour-dough yeast I had brought back from one of my concert trips to San Francisco. She did not eat butter, but I managed to find some *prieselbeeren* jam, which she loved enormously. She took no alcohol at all except the sherry that went into her bean soup. She had two cooks in the house who doubled in brass as serving maids and clean-up women. But no one ever touched her laboratory.

"It's a little dusty," she said, "but I know where everything is, and a small mistake with a bottle of developer might be catastrophic."

She had a German-born chauffeur, who was also her handy-man. He was, as I remember, the kind of chauffeur who drove much too fast, and dominating the road as he did, he was constantly in trouble with other more timid drivers, who, not understanding his bawling and baying (he spoke English with certain difficulties), usually pulled over and allowed the oversize Lincoln to weave its way through the traffic.

This man was extraordinarily accurate with an automobile, and drove through many dangerous situations quite calmly. In his early days, in German Silesia, he had been a chauffeur to a German general. This had been on the Russian front in the first World War. As he grew older, he continued to use the Germany-army method of doing things. I might add that as I was a slightly crippled veteran of the same war, he and I were not overly friendly. All this amused Miss Ulmann greatly.

Miss Ulmann had a dressmaker, who had served her apprentice-ship in Paris. As a result, Doris wore fabulously beautiful clothes. She even managed to wear beautiful hats, and never went out bare-headed. Besides all this, she employed a dress consultant from Altman's. This fine gentleman moonlighted himself into quite a tidy sum each month, advising her on suits, coats, tweed items, etc. She was very fond of tweeds, and she demanded that if I was to be seen with her, I must not look like a Greenwich Village drifter. So I moved into tweeds almost at once.

After her death we discovered, in what I had thought to be a wine-closet, more than 50 pairs of shoes, many of which had never been worn. In disposing of these shoes we had quite a problem because her feet were so small. If my memory serves me, her shoes came from a custom boot-maker who had a tiny shop on 48th Street just off Fifth Avenue. After I had deposited her at the shoe-shop I would walk over to the Church of St. Mary the Virgin and pray fervently for Doris and her recovery from the malaise she suffered continually. When I returned to the shoe-maker's, there would be Doris with a collection of shoe-boxes, looking like some dark-complexioned princess from one of the southern European countries.

Doris Ulmann never slept well, and as the modern sleeping-pills were yet to be developed, she took what her doctors prescribed and sat up much of the night with her photography. Her desire to work at night complicated my job greatly, for my own tendency was to work in the daytime and sleep at night.

As I have already said, the theatre fascinated her enormously, and as I grew to be her constant companion, I naturally went with her to the opera, ballet, puppet-shows and the best of the current New York plays. As soon as we appeared in the theatre lobby there would be a collection of ticket-scalpers and other wise-guys who would make belittling remarks about "that Johnnie Niles who, in spite of the Depression, seems to have everything going his way. Miss Ulmann has him handy to pick her up in case she falls down..."

Once she did fall down, and I picked her up and helped her to her seat. She patted my hand and said: "What did that swine say as we came in the building?" I told her I did not know, as I usually did on such occasions, wanting to shield her as much as I could. "Thanks," she said. "I'll be your friend some day."

I was constantly picking up her belongings when she dropped her enormous hand-bag, either on the street or in a public building, and we always had a laugh over the variety of unnecessary objects she carried. And when we were traveling through the southern mountains, I carried her over streams of water and once was photographed giving her a piggyback lift over Cutshine Creek.

In 1926 she had a bad fall not far from her home. Her knee-cap was broken, and she had to lie in a hospital for a long time recovering. This accident colored the remainder of her life because, afterward, she walked rather heavily on a cane, and, being such a proud person, she resented this disability. I ultimately became her cane: we would rehearse walking without "the blooming cane," going around and around her lovely drawing-room, being extra careful at the turns. It was a process I understood very well, for I had also walked on a cane for quite a few years after a German anti-aircraft gunner got my range in France, not far from Laon. But Doris was never able to walk without some small assistance after her fall.

After that her dresses were almost floor-length, and they were particularly attractive to the female-persons she encountered in the South. She wore filmy summer dresses because she said she suffered from the heat of our southern states. The local women, particularly the ones who lived far from the towns and the high roads, loved her lacy summer things and would touch the cloth, admire the way it was sewn and put together. At first, Doris would offer to have a similar dress sent to the admirer, but what pleased them most was a proposal to let the original dress be worn sometime. I do not remember that anyone ever took her up on her offer, but they were all greatly pleased by the idea.

During the summer of 1933—it was the summer of the dotted-Swiss dresses—we worked in and around Murphy, N. C. Her lovely white dresses were sent to the laundry every day, and she would always tip the laundress generously, besides paying the company its regular fee. I remember one of the Negro laundresses referring to Doris as "that white angel with the black eyes."

On our trips to the South Miss Ulmann carried two cameras, one an 8x10, the other $6\frac{1}{2}$x$8\frac{1}{2}$. They were what we called view cameras, and neither of them had a shutter. Exposure was made by removing and replacing the lens-cap. Both cameras used glass plates. There was also a 4x5 in her luggage, but it was referred to as "Johnnie's camera." And although I used it very seldom, I did get several good shots of Doris Ulmann working. This smaller camera used cut film.

We usually carried about 10 boxes of $6\frac{1}{2}$x$8\frac{1}{2}$ glass plates. Not too many plates for the 8x10 camera went with us, because this larger camera was just too cumbersome to take out on field trips. Along with this, there was a large box containing liquids and trays, and a bolt of cloth to cover up hotel windows and make her room into a kind of darkroom. Miss Ulmann usually took two adjoining rooms in the hotels where we stayed, one to serve as a darkroom and one as her sleeping quarters. And although she decided quite early in our travels that it was too complicated to develop while on the road, she still needed the darkroom to get the glass plates into their wooden holders.

All the photographic equipment, along with many containers of clothing and food, packed the car to the cloth top. The car was an oversized Lincoln, with an enormous baggage compartment attached to the back. It was driven exclusively by the German chauffeur; I never touched it. My own car was a Chevrolet sedan, and it went into places where a mule would hardly be caught.

I remember so well the time I started over a rather rickety-looking bridge. Suddenly I felt the bridge creaking under us. I quickly backed up, and as I did, the entire bridge collapsed and fell into a gorge about 50 feet deep. Doris covered her eyes with her hand and wept hysterically. Afterward we agreed that a mule would not have made such a mistake. The mule would have looked first.

The German chauffeur never took the Lincoln into such situations. In fact, he usually remained in one of the larger cities, cooling his heels, eating three meals a day and being a great gentleman, while I drove the Chevrolet on the "one-hundred-and-eleven roads" (roads that do not appear on any map) where we did the photography and where I recorded folk songs. (When I say "recording," I mean writing down with pencil and paper, because I never had mechanical devices of any kind to take down my folk-music discoveries.)

So Miss Ulmann depended on us all, for whatever we could do, except in the matter of photography. This was her area and hers exclusively. If I ever assisted her, she stood over me, watching every move I made, telling me forty times how to do the simplest of things —how to pick up the unexposed glass plates and put them in the plate-holders, how to handle the developer and fix the photographs when they came out of the developing bath. She mixed all her own chemicals; no one assisted her in this.

The developing process, of course, took place in the New York apartment. Doris was a night-time person; I was not. About midnight I would get weary and say: "All right, Doris. This is all for today." And I would unroll a bedroll I kept in one corner of the laboratory and go to sleep. She would keep right on working until the very early hours. Whenever she quit work, I would wake up and start the hot water for her first cup of morning coffee.

In the theatre oft-times, at concerts or at the rare evening parties we attended, she would get sleepy and nod, and I would nudge her and wake her up.

"You awful person," she would say, "why didn't you let me take a little nap? I didn't get but two hours of sleep last night."

"Well," I said, "whose fault was that?"

"Yours, of course. You're supposed to be the smart one in this enterprise."

And we would laugh over that. We laughed a lot—over snapshot photography, which she held in complete derision, over the fact that I was not producing enough music, etc., etc.... She enjoyed bantering with me, and I think that was why she put up with me: because she could tease me and I understood it was affectionate teasing.

Her sense of humor was on the bitter side, and she had absolutely no patience with stupidity. In the southern mountains she dealt with people who knew very little about the ways of the world, and who had in most cases a minimum of education, but they had native intelligence. And they were the grist to her photographic mill.

Doris had had all the educational advantages available in New York City. She had traveled abroad extensively in her early days with her father (her mother had died). She spoke German and French fluently, Italian very well. Her English was flawless.

I used to tease her occasionally about having a Brooklyn accent. This was a sore point, and she said that before I made comment on her accent, I had better adjust my own, because, she said, I sounded sometimes like a camp-meeting preacher or a southern politician trying to make a pitch for a few votes. But it was all in fun.

Miss Ulmann's point of view about the people she photographed was quite simple. She concluded that there would always be someone handy with a snapshot camera to photograph the pretty girls with frilly dresses and curled hair, with made-up eyes and lips. She was not concerned with these people, but rather with those who were downright, genuine individuals. A person had to be a character, more or less, before she became interested.

She photographed a great many doctors, lawyers and judges. She photographed scientists, musicians and actors; farmers and loggers; drovers and moonshiners; she even photographed me, endlessly and affectionately. She said she had to get to know a person first. She believed that all the people she photographed had one thing in common—a quality that could be called genuineness. But of all the people she photographed I believe the ones she loved most were the old mountaineers with white whiskers, the patriarchal types, and their ancient wives, though she also made many photos of young mountain men and women and their endless children. It was, however, in the faces of the old men and women that she saw what attracted her the most—the care and trouble of their lives, but also the ultimate serenity. To record their images she was prepared to do hours of work.

Doris Ulmann worked with great deliberation and care. Every picture was composed. She never used a light-meter. "I am the light-meter," she would say. Neither of her cameras had a shutter. She would remove the lens-cap, count, replace it. In the course of a full working day she would make a maximum of 20 exposures. It was my job to carry the glass plates in their holders—10 slung over one shoulder, 10 over the other.

She philosophized with her subjects as she worked, and I wrote down almost everything that was said. She was greatly amused at drunks who came up to her and called her "honey" and "sugarfoot." These people she photographed quickly—before they could wander away. They were relaxed, and their faces told a tremendous story.

She was willing to put up with any kind of weather, sticky heat or rain, or any kind of discomfort—poor beds and food—for the sake of getting to some remote spot where some ancient sage and his woman-person might be found sitting in front of their cabin. And if the sage had a shock of white hair and a beard, her joy was complete.

They actually seemed to have been waiting for her. Inside their dark cabins they would be working at the spinning wheel, the younger women sitting at the loom or carding wool for the older ones. The children might be pulling weeds in the tobacco beds or later in the season, when the crop had been cut, gathering flines to be tied later in small bundles and sold with the rest of the crop.

All these things fascinated her. These were the people she wanted to record for posterity. She feared they were disappearing. She was right up to a certain point. They are thinning out, but some of them will always remain, and now though more of them move out of the mountains and into the cities, I find that many of them are exactly as they were in 1930. They are turning out to be the same kind of white-haired old men and women, and even though they are disturbed by radio and television, they are really not much different from their fabulous grandfathers and grandmothers.

One thing I am proud to report: although we went into places where outsiders were seldom seen, no one ever shot at us.

The Fugate Stir-Off is an example. At first, I could not understand why so many men were needed to do such a small job. A stir-off is merely a stirring off, or removal, of the scum from the top of boiling sorghum. The result is a clear, syrupy residue usually called "sorghums," in the plural, by the mountain people. It is their substitute for maple syrup.

The sorghum plant is a little shorter than a corn-stalk. It is cut either by hand or by a mowing machine and is fed into a press motivated by mule power. Around and around the mule walks, and from the press comes a thin, watery juice, which is caught in buckets and later boiled down. As children, we used to cut the stalks and chew them. The juice was sweet and watery, and usually gave us a bad case of diarrhea.

Of course, we were anxious to photograph the stir-off process, but Miss Ulmann was having difficulty. She finally called me over and asked me to look through her ground glass. There were flashes of light coming through the lense. It was not sunlight or someone playing tricks with a mirror. No, it was something else...So I went over to the source of the light and found about twenty-five well-oiled and loaded rifles.

Miss Ulmann spoke to one of the younger men and asked if they could move the rifles.

"No, miss," he said very politely, "we can't remove them 'cause at a stir-off you simply can't go around without the protection of a good, straight-shooting gun-rifle."

Miss Ulmann offered to have me rub a little mud on the barrels to cut the glare, but that suggestion was not received with much enthusiasm. So we moved the camera far enough to one side to miss the flash of the rifle-barrels. And the stir-off photos were very successful after that.

I remember once we were crossing Cutshine Creek near Hyden, Ky. (Cutshine is a way of saying "cut shin." Tradition has it that a man fell in this very rocky creek and injured himself badly. And as the years passed the words Cut-Shin Creek became Cutshine Creek.) The creek at this point was wide and shallow. So I picked up Doris on my back and started to piggy-back her to the other side. We had gotten no more than halfway across when Doris said: "Let's go back, back to where we started." We set up the camera. There was a boy handy. She focused the camera and then showed the boy exactly how to remove the lens-cap, count to three and put the cap back. "Now let's start across again," she said to me. "We're going to get a photograph of this operation." Doris Ulmann had a tremendous sense of theatre. She saw drama when it was coming.

So I picked her up again and started across the creek a second time. When we reached the middle of the creek, we stopped and she signalled the boy to remove the cap and count to three. He did exactly as he was told. With this accomplished, I continued my trip, deposited Miss Ulmann on the far side safely, then went back across the creek to turn the plate-holder around and deliver the camera back to her. The picture was later developed, and it turned out to be a delightful thing, Doris Ulmann riding piggy-back across Cutshine Creek.

Unfortunately, we did not get a photo of me carrying her across a muddy ditch in my arms. This was not far from Pine Mountain School. We were trying to photograph a marvelous old man, who had his own private coal-mine. He mined the coal himself and carried it in small coal-buckets right to his own fireplace. He also sold a small part of his output and in this way, supported himself. He told us that as he lived alone, he got along quite nicely on his coal sales.

I carried Doris across the muddy ditch and back again, and in the process almost ruined my clothes. A few days later several boxes of new clothes appeared as if by magic, and Doris took my battered suit and shoes and gave them to one of the local boys.

Near Gatlinburg, Tenn. we had a somewhat similar experience, except that my life and the life of one of our horses was endangered. We had climbed a treacherous narrow pathway, both mounted, and did get some very fine shots of a local bee-man and his wife and his bee-hives. Several bees tried to bite me, but I managed to chase them away with a wide-brimmed hat. Bees seem to have a tendency to bite the top of the head. They also attacked Doris, but her thick hair protected her. Finally, we had all the exposures we wanted, so we packed up our gear and started down the mountain in the direction of Gatlinburg.

Doris had procured a handsome, if somewhat impractical, pair of jodhpurs from her tailor in New York, and in this outfit she rode like the Queen of Sheba. I followed behind, carrying the camera, a tripod, a package of food (against our getting lost), two heavy bags of plates and a box of extra lenses. All went well until my horse, somewhat overloaded, made a miss-step to the right and fell down the side of the mountain, through bushes and briars. Having ridden quite a bit in my youth, I knew enough to get my feet out of the stirrups. Hugging our precious photographic material, I finally landed on a rock ledge. My clothes were in shreds, but the equipment was intact. I called to Doris to ride on down to the hotel and round up a rescue team to extricate me. It seemed an awfully long time before they finally came, but soon after that they managed to haul me back up to the path, which was about a hundred feet above the spot where I had landed. The rescue-team was rather amused. They had seen me earlier in the day, strutting around in my "ridin' pants." Now I had no pants at all.

I recovered from my wounds in about 36 hours. Meanwhile, a local doctor had wisely given me an anti-tetanus shot, which caused me to break out in the most fantastic red spots. Doris's sense of humor came to our rescue. She said I had obviously come down with one of the

Unfortunate Diseases. In a few days an entire new outfit of clothing arrived, and also a new watch, which I am wearing to this day. I think I should add that the unfortunate horse had to be destroyed.

All this will give the reader some idea of the trouble to which Doris Ulmann would go in order to get what she wanted in the way of photography and legend. It was not all as near-tragic as the Gatlinburg episode. Most of it was easy and delightfully amusing. For example we would pull up in front of a house, beside a newly-paved road, and explain to the occupants that we had come to take their pictures. In a moment's time they would be lined in a row, looking their smiling best.

It was quite easy, after the first round of photography, to get the women to put on their grannies' linsey-woolsey dresses, and then they would go into the attics or lean-to sheds and produce spinning wheels and portions of looms and some wool-cards. They would gladly show us how their ancestors carried on, and then we would photograph them in these magnificent costumes. At Pine Mountain Settlement School we got four of the prettiest girls to dress in some linsey-woolseys and pose in front of their cabin. One of these girls later turned out to be an eminent doctor in Baltimore, and the others became school-teachers. Pine Mountain was a treasure-trove for us. We photographed many interesting people there, and I took down some wonderful folk-ballads meanwhile.

Miss Ulmann never paid anyone to pose for her, and I followed her advice in the area of folk-ballad collecting, up to a certain point. (Or she may have been following my advice; I am not certain at this late date.) However, she did promise her subjects copies of their photographs, and made good on her promises. I can remember delivering hundreds of photos in person in North Carolina and Kentucky after her death. In New York City we were photographing a fruit-stand, the owner of which suggested to Miss Ulmann that she give her daughter $20 for the purchase of some shoes. Miss Ulmann was outraged. We quickly packed up the camera and took our leave.

Pennsylvania provided us with some great subjects. We photographed graveyards, churches, schoolhouses and the wonderful dairy barns. Doris loved the idea of children going to school in those narrow, horse-drawn buggies, and we photographed them. We spent several weeks in Pennsylvania, and it was a real experience.

In the early 1930's we went up to Boston. There we photographed Harvard dons, Calvin Coolidge and Mrs. Coolidge. Photographing Calvin Coolidge was very easy: he sat perfectly still and never said a word. Durgin Park restaurant, Faneuil Hall and the vegetable markets in the area supplied us with some good shots. We naturally went to Durgin Park for lunch, and I took the menu top to bottom. Miss Ulmann stuck to Indian pudding and coffee.

Miss Ulmann always asked her subjects what they did in the way of work and if they liked working. I remember one elderly leather-tanner who lived and worked in North Carolina. He was in the process of curing and tanning a collection of calf-hides when we called on him.

"How do you like your job?" Miss Ulmann said.

"I don't dread hit a little bit," came the answer.

He it was who gave me a long, detailed account of how to tan leather. It would take 45 minutes of the reader's time to read it, so suffice it to say that one phrase kept coming back in his narrative—

"dependin' on the weather". The number of hours the hides lay in the tanning solution, the amount of sunlight, the number of licks the hide received to knock off the hair—all these things were highly variable, "dependin' on the weather".

In those days, the early 1930's, blacksmiths still used leather bellows to fan their fires. Also in North Carolina, we ran onto a pair of people, a tanner and a blacksmith, who were making a bellows from pieces of leather about 6 feet in length to activate a huge forge. Both men claimed to be part Meulungeon—that is, descendants of the Lost Tribe of Virginia. We also photographed some very lovely Meulungeon women.

One of our most interesting experiences was a mounted trip to a little settlement called Grassy Valley. It was located near the boundary between Tennessee and North Carolina. We left Asheville and drove about an hour and a half to a point called Barlow's Store, where we picked up a pair of horses. Miss Ulmann's mount was thoroughly docile, but mine was determined to unhorse me, and almost succeeded when we passed a side-delivery rake drawn by three mules. As usual, I was disadvantaged by carrying a great load of photographic equipment.

But we finally made it up to Grassy Valley, and there we encountered a remarkable old lady more than 100 years of age. In her early days, she had lived through many Indian battles, and her great-grandson, who seemed to be her constant companion, teased her about having had a "Red Indian boy-friend."

We photographed her carding, spinning and weaving, with her

delightful and handsome great-grandson sitting at the loom with her. She told us that she sold a considerable crop of wool every year in Asheville. In spite of her age, she did all the carding and spinning of this wool herself. She also said that the Asheville purchasers in turn sold the wool to some weavers in the Hebrides. Whether this was true or not, I cannot say. But I did discover that the Asheville buyers paid well for the wool.

Miss Ulmann had wanted to take a present to this fine old lady, so before starting on our trip we had bought an inexpensive hand-bag at Barlow's Store and had filled it with such articles as a ball of twine, some cotton gloves, a pair of scissors, some vaseline, some aspirin tablets, a box of soda, some baking powder, a small bottle of Jockey Club perfume, some adhesive tape and a small bottle of what they called Arnica. All this, as I recall, came to about $1.75. Of course, this was during the depression when $1.75 bought a lot of things.

The old lady reacted as a child under a Christmas-tree. It was pure delight to see her open the bag and take the things out, one at a time. There were gales of laughter from the family and cries of delight from the old lady.

The trip to Grassy Valley, as I remember it, did not yield any music, but many of our other trips did. Doris Ulmann was very patient on such occasions, giving me time to pursue my own research. She also developed an attitude of great kindness to my strange ways— my continual search for good food, my unwillingness to stay up late, and my desire to write down everything anybody said. I carried a small black notebook and some pages of score-paper on all our trips.

Although Doris Ulmann loved music, I believe she considered me a bit daft because I wanted to stop the car every time I heard a sound that remotely resembled music. If we came upon some young people dancing to banjo or guitar accompaniment, we were certain to stop, because the guitar music was important to me and the dancers were usually interested in being photographed.

But photographing moving dancers with Doris's lens-cap technique was difficult. She was at her best in character-study portraits of people whom she posed with great care. She also excelled in still photography, and did some wonderful pin-holes. For this I made her a set of copper plates, which she slipped into the lens-board in place of the lens. They had graduated holes in them, some as small as 128th of an inch. I engaged a jeweler to drill the very small ones, and I did the others myself.

This type of photography is very simple indeed. You aim the camera at the scene (it is invariably landscapes or buildings), you pull out the plate-guard and allow the camera to stand completely still for 20 minutes to a half-hour. The results are astounding; the pictures are actually stereoscopic in effect.

Doris thought that photography started with the pin-hole technique, rather than with complicated lenses. She once tried to "pin-hole" a recumbent cow. But the cow decided to get up for a drink of water, and the plate was spoiled. Doris loved photographing animals—horses, mules, oxen—even though it took endless time and trouble for her to do so since she used time-exposures exclusively. One second was probably the shortest time she ever used. I once tried to get her to photograph a particularly lovely Siamese cat, but the cat would not sit still.

As I said before, Miss Ulmann moved about the country in a large Lincoln automobile, except for the short excursions over rough roads, which were generally made in my car. She carried boxes and boxes of glass plates, which had to be put into plate-holders. (This was why she had an extra room as a darkroom in the hotels where we stayed.) At one point, in Berea College, she did a little developing, but we found it was too time-consuming. So two or three times in each season she would send her car and her chauffeur back to New York to deliver boxes of exposed plates to her laboratory.

Miss Ulmann seldom spoiled a plate. I can remember a few, but very few indeed. This was because of her great deliberateness. She went about everything carefully and slowly, thinking everything out in advance. There was no hurry-up and no snap-shot business. She was greatly opposed to the idea of the snap-shot. However, as time passed and the new German cameras came on the market, I yearned for one. Thereupon she sent up north and got the best Rolleiflex to be had. Along with this came a wonderful light-meter, one of Mr. Weston's best.

Doris immediately looked upon me as a complete faker. Up to that time I had been using a 4x5 camera with either cut film or DC ortho plates, and I think I was doing some nice things. But when I went to toying with the snap-shot camera she put me down at the bottom of the page.

But her illness was catching up with her, and she became less and less able to move around in our rugged country. That was when I began to take over many of the tasks. I would set up and focus the camera, arrange the subjects and ask Doris if she wanted to check on me.

She would say wearily: "Go on and expose it. You don't always give the impression of being very smart, but I think you've got pretty good sense, and of course I'm very fond of you. Go on and expose the plate."

In that way I took many of her shots just before the end of her life, and as I look at the prints (I have seen hundreds of them recently) some seem quite good. Of course, Doris Ulmann was sitting in the shade, watching me work, smiling at my stumbling ways and saying: "If these shots don't come off, I'll invent a new way of telling you about your errors."

But she didn't live long enough to do any of these things because she died August 28th, 1934, and some of the exposures of 1933 and all of those of 1934 were developed after her death.

The last day of our working life together was spent on the top of Turkey Mountain, not far from Asheville, N. C. First we started "to the top of Turkey" and on the way photographed a farmer topping and suckering his tobacco crop. While Doris did the photographing, I took down a nearly complete version of one of our great ballads, and later we got a picture of the ballad-singer standing in the midst of the tobacco plants.

As we moved up the hill from the tobacco patch, my car slipped off the road. It had rained the night before, and the mud road was slick. I had a bad time getting the car back on the road, and all this excitement bothered Doris greatly.

Finally we got to the Top of Turkey, where we had been expected since early in the day. Doris was obviously in pain and near collapse. Our hosts were very understanding. A white-bearded grandfather produced a very tasty kind of drink, and I encouraged Doris to take some of it. It proved to be wild-cherry bounce. After the first few sips Doris went on and drank the entire glass. In all my years of working with her I had never seen her drink an alcoholic beverage. But the cherry bounce cheered her up mightily. She even ate some food, much to everyone's delight.

The dinner-table was laden with every kind of food available in that part of the country. Children stood behind each guest with a fly-brush, usually a small limb off a pine-tree, and cunningly swept the flies away. This was called fly-bushing. I made up for Miss Ulmann's lack of appetite. The food was wonderful, and I ate inordinately. I remember they had three kinds of dessert and store-bought cookies besides.

After dinner we took some photos, but Doris grew less and less able to carry on. I put her in the car and slowly we started down the road, which was in fact a trail and a slick one at that. On the way we came across another man who had slipped off the road. As I remember, he had a pick-up truck loaded with women and children. It took a team of mules quite a bit of time to set him to rights again, so we could move on. Finally, I got her back to the Battery Park Hotel. Her eyes were half closed, she had a terrifying gray look about her, and she was muttering about cars and mud. That was the end of her life really. She never picked up a camera again.

Her nurse came to her room and started to keep a chart on her condition. (Because of Doris's failing health, this woman had come down with us from New York.) But a half-hour after that a Viennese doctor and his beautiful wife came to ask if we would be guests at a gala dinner they were giving that evening. I explained the situation as well as I could, and the doctor gave Doris some mild stimulant.

It worked like magic. Here was Doris, an hour later, dressed in the most beautiful clothes she could find in her wardrobe trunk, and together we went out to the Viennese doctor's party. It was in celebration of someone's birthday, as I recall. The evening had a strange, dream-like quality. Doris sat in a high chair that looked like a throne. She smiled wanly. I stood beside her and tried ever so hard to smile too, but it was no good. Our smiles were less than skin-deep.

Later I went out to the car and unpacked my largest dulcimer. Then I sang as I had never sung before, and Doris, dear thing that she was, fell asleep. Finally, I decided that we must bid our hosts farewell and get Doris home and to bed. I did get her back to the hotel and with the assistance of a couple of bellboys, into her room. Her nurse came and put her to bed. She said that Miss Ulmann must be taken to her doctor. Her fever was up and her pulse was erratic.

I called New York and discovered that her doctor was in Scranton, Pa. on vacation. We left Asheville that very night. Doris was curled up on the seat beside me. Occasionally she would wake up and ask me if I was still awake. All the while the nurse and chauffeur were packing and preparing for an early morning departure. Her determination to travel in my car was quite touching. "I'll ride home with Johnnie Niles," she said, "and I don't want to hear any more about it."

It was a dismal trip. I remember once upon an afternoon we stopped near that beautiful little city of Winston-Salem. I lifted her out of the car and sat her down on a log beside the road. "Let us rest here a while," she said. "This is as good a place to die as any I've seen in a long time."

I got her into the car and drove a few miles to a village where there was a nice filling-station with a well-furnished rest-room. I carried her into the rest-room and encouraged her to lie down on the couch. Some Negroes passed and in response to some joke they were recounting, they laughed and laughed. Then one of them looked into the rest-room and saw Miss Ulmann's gray face. The laugh stopped at once. It was as if someone had cut a piece of magnetic tape. The laugh just hung in the air. Doris had the look of death in her face.

I got her to Scranton as quickly as I could. There her doctor examined her and told me to take her to New York at once, where she could have the very best of care. But all the king's horses and all the king's men could not put her back together again. She died quietly in the early morning of August 28th, 1934.

Doris Ulmann attended the Clarence White School of Photography, and there in two years learned how to manage the camera and how to mix and employ her chemicals. But basically she was self-taught, for she was a genuine artist and as such, had to find her own way. She was a completely remarkable woman and one who gave her life, and as much of her estate as was necessary, to the idea of photographing simple Americans.

John Jacob Niles
Boot Hill Farm, Lexington, Kentucky

The Photographs

3

5

7

10

11

15

16

18

21

22

23

25

29

33

34

39

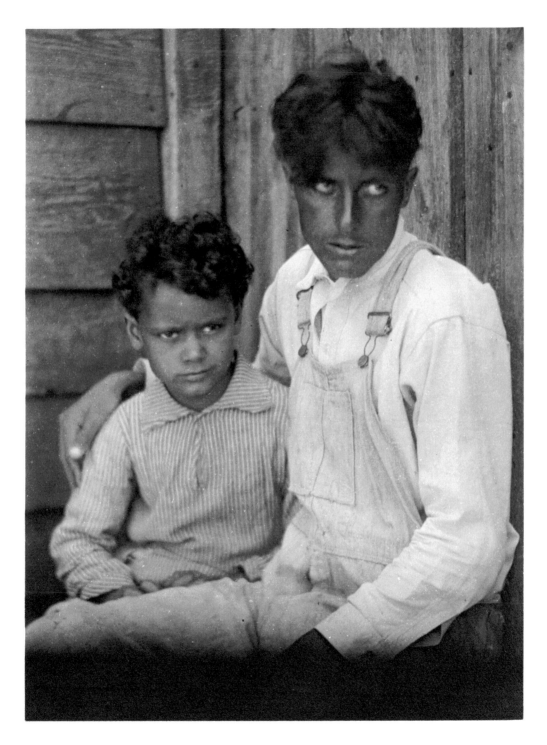

41

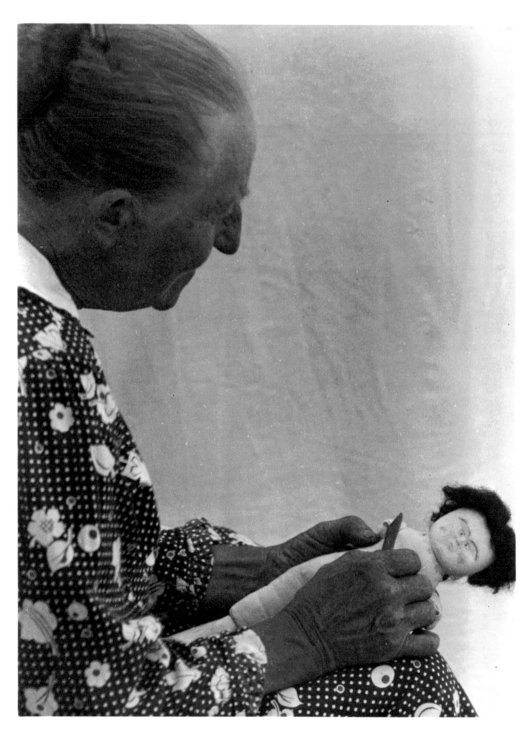

43

45

46

49

50

51

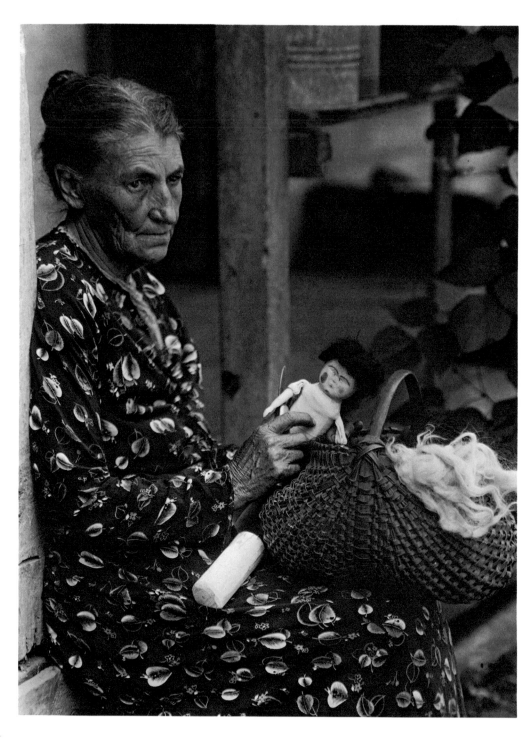

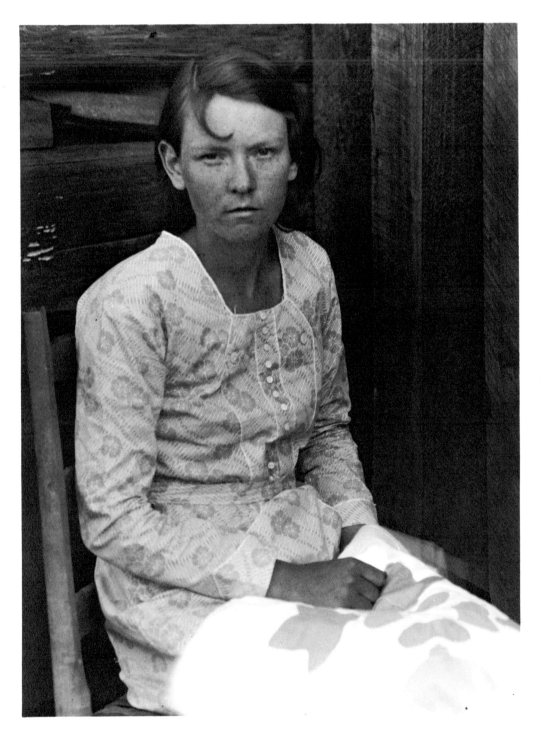

59

60

61

"IS IT REALLY NECESSARY THAT WE KNOW ONE TO HAVE BEEN NAMED SMITH AND ANOTHER CALLED JONES? WITH THE EXCEPTION OF THE VERY YOUNG, THEY ARE ALL SURELY DEAD."

John Jacob Niles

An Identification of the Plates,
With Comments, by John Jacob Niles:

Plate 3:   *An unknown preacher (the box under his arm contained his Bible and some small personal articles).*

Plate 5:   *W. J. Martin, Brasstown, North Carolina. He farmed and supplemented his income by woodcarving.*

Plate 7:   *An unnamed member of the Holiness sect.*

Plate 8:   *John Alexander Meadows. He operated a gristmill near Pine Log, North Carolina.*

Plate 9:   *A coal-miner.*

Plate 11:   *J. O. Penland. Farmer, Brasstown, North Carolina.*

Plate 12:   *Christopher Lewis. Preacher, Wooton, Kentucky.*

Plate 15:   *Mr. Ritchie, Viper, Kentucky. He was the father of a large family, including folksinger Jean Ritchie. His wife is shown in Plate 42.*

Plate 17:   *A Pennsylvania fireman.*

Plate 19:   *Mrs. Lowery, Brasstown, North Carolina.*